SEASONS OF THE HEART

ALAN SPENCE is an award-winning novelist, playwright and short story writer, described as 'one of Scotland's most accomplished literary talents' (*The Times*). Awards include the People's Prize, Macallan *Scotland on Sunday* Prize, McVitie Prize (Scottish Writer of the Year) and TMA Martini Award. Glasgow-born, he is based in Edinburgh and is currently writer-in-residence at the University of Aberdeen.

also by Alan Spence

for Issbel & Bob

SEASONS
OF
THE
HEART

with much love

HAIKU *& gratitude*

alan

ALAN SPENCE

alan Spence

Sep. 2000

CANONGATE

First published in Great Britain in 2000 by
Canongate Books Ltd,
14 High Street Edinburgh EH1 1TE

10 9 8 7 6 5 4 3 2 1

Copyright © Alan Spence, 2000

The moral rights of the author have been asserted

The publishers gratefully acknowledge subsidy from the
Scottish Arts Council towards the publication of this volume

British Library Cataloguing-in-Publication Data
A catalogue record for this book is available on
request from the British Library

ISBN 1 84195 052 1

Typeset by Forge Design
Printed and bound by WS Bookwell, Finland

To
CKG

ACKNOWLEDGEMENTS

Some of these poems have appeared in the following publications:

Akros, Atoms of Delight (Morning Star), *Best of Scottish Poetry* (Chambers), *Fox, Henry, Glasgow Herald, Glasgow Review, Glasgow University Magazine, Lines Review, OAR, Oasis, Pack of Cards* (Aberdeen Libraries), *Poetry Glasgow, Rebel Inc Magazine, Scotsman, Scottish Poetry 5* (EUP), *Skinklin Star, Words Magazine, Writers in Brief* (Book Trust)

first warmth of spring
I feel as if
I have been asleep

first warmth of spring
under cracking ice
the jawbone of a dog

crocuses
where last week
the snow lay thick

the spring breeze –
the paper flowers also
tremble

into the sea I launch
a piece of driftwood –
with great ceremony!

spring rain
a yellow oil-drum
bobbing down the river

dog rolling daft on the grass
beside the first daffodils
of the year

this spring evening
blue estuary light
vast empty sky

trying to talk
we can only laugh and point –
sun glinting on the loch

fourteen donkeys
in a field
fourteen donkeys!

the puppy
ferociously challenging
a daffodil

that old/new
smell of fresh
cut grass

morning meditation
clouds lift clear
from the mountain top

sunlight through stained glass
fragrance of oranges
the sound of a bell

the flowering plant nods
acknowledging
my gaze

two swallows
dip and soar
making a summer

the yellow gorse
making the sky
more blue

the whole sky and more
reflected in each raindrop
hanging from that branch

rainmist over loch and hills
I peer but cannot see
the other shore

blind man on a park bench,
the flowers,
their faces to the sun

country road
too dark to see the flowers
but their scent is yellow

yellowlantern tendrils,
I've just found out your name –
hello laburnum!

using a peach
for a paperweight –
summer breeze

a few wild flowers
placed in an old pot
grace our temporary home

three tethered rowing-boats
bobbing on a pond –
summer rain

statue of christ, the sun
behind his head –
butterfly opens its wings

puffed-up cloud
the swan's feathers ruffled
white sails on the lake

camomile flowers –
a whole garden
in the bottom of my cup

sun on her bare head
she carries
a hat-full of plums

the grass is so very green
the poppies are
so very very red

a single cloud
and its shadow
on the flat blue sea

a child's rope swing hangs
limp from a tree –
mid-day heat

midsummer midnight
full moon in the pale sky
over the north sea

patter of rain on the tent roof
an ant
crawling over my hand

sagging pot belly
of the old pit pony –
summer heat

a feast for this fly,
the crumbs from my bread –
look at him rubbing his hands!

swiping at these flies
I could kill them all –
the hot sticky afternoon

don't dart away so quick
little lizard
I didn't mean to scare you

summer downpour –
the pregnant cat
enduring it

african rain drumming
marimba rhythm
on the iron roof

a tree on fire
against the blazing
sunset sky

the mark of my boot
in the clay
has gathered rainwater
overnight

confetti
scattered on the pavement
wet by the rain

valleys, mountains and rivers –
the chance patterns weathered
on this stone wall

children
dipping sticks in a puddle
drawing pictures
that dry and fade

rainbows
in the spray kicked up
by the lorry

chanting aum
first light
the hills take shape

the zen garden –
a crack on the wall
in exactly the right place

the zen garden –
I too
am included

the master's footprints
along the old
dirt road

the moon moves with us
as we walk,
drifts from tree to tree

the cat swipes at the breeze,
shadow-boxing with
nothing-I-can-see

summer evening –
through the open window,
an old song

vague shapes in the halflight
the cry of a bat
the rising moon is red

the familiarity
of everything
under tonight's moon

what am I thinking?
'the sound of the water' –
the sound of the water

look *slowly* he says
and you'll see it –
eclipse of the moon

warming my feet
in the patch of sunlight
on the floor

a sweet peach
but the last bite
is bitter

the sun in the water
jiggles on the end of
the fisherman's line

the rain has stopped
the sky is clear
come out and look
at the stars

field on the cliff-top
the horse's mane lifts
in the wind off the sea

sudden gust –
the seagull scudding
backwards

small boat on the loch,
far off hills faintly
blue through mist

a single petal falls,
touches the tamboura string –
a tiny *pang*

suddenly shivering
my clothes are too thin –
the first yellowing leaf

the scarecrow
holds his arms out,
shows off his new coat

someone has given
a warm scarf
to the scarecrow

the dark field
puddles reflect back
the last light

crossing the bridge –
the other side
is lost in mist

behind a skull
in the junkshop window
smiling buddha

japanese landscapes
in the damp patch
on the ceiling

soaking in the hot tub –
cold rain battering
on the roof

the darkening sky –
a bird hovers over
the flooded field

chained to its post
the guard-dog barks
at the pouring rain

carefully
cleaning between the toes
of the buddha

along the highway
through Connecticut,
stink of a dead skunk

one for sorrow –
she waves at the magpie
to break its spell

high winds tonight
the clouds stand still
the stars go scudding past

three seals on a rock
tails up, drying off –
september sun

an apple rotting
just where it fell
the smell of autumn

pawprint of a dog
in the concrete
of the sidewalk

just an autumn evening
why these tears?
just an autumn evening

all this ache in my heart –
sound of the wind
in the pines

edge of the ocean
heron balanced
on one leg

autumn cold
the cat's rough tongue
on the back of my hand

the willow tree
I had never noticed
before this grey rainy day

damp leaves drift to earth
the sun hangs tangled
in the branches of a tree

sipping tea
burning incense
listening to the rain

red on red –
fall of dead leaves
on rusting scrap

all my life
and again now –
this full moon

between the silhouetted
chimney-pots
a single star

the door bangs back
on its hinges
and in come the leaves

another city square
and dead leaves falling –
I am far from home

I know I will die
but still ...
the full round moon

the sound of a woman's
mop and bucket
on the chapel's cold stone floor

see the wind?
she says
as it shakes the trees

catch its reflection
in my cup – take a sip,
I'm drinking the moon!

wading
ankle-deep
through fallen leaves

the borrowed umbrella
we are sharing –
a few small holes in it

as if there was nothing else
the tick of the clock
rain on the window

up through the floorboards
smell of my neighbour's house –
cigarettes and onions

rain falling
especially
on me

the sound of the rain
the sound of the rain
the sound of the rain

grey earth sea sky
taking flight the heron
stabs the void

first one solitary star
then one by one they pierce
the darkening sky

after the fireworks
cold and still
the moon

wind tugs at the tree
till the last leaf
lets go

400 miles from my friends
the apples they gave me
for the journey

the sound of the cold –
a knife-blade being sharpened
on stone

the tiny cloud of
the cat's breath
on the windowpane

the last leaves,
the first snow,
falling

beginning of winter
in the chill
of the milk-bottles

winter again –
on the thinnest of branches
a tiny bird is perched

the cold wind
rattles the bones
of the scarecrow

all there is?
stink of sick
on the latenight bus

shielding my eyes
from the streetlamps' glare
to look at the stars

after the nightshift
sparkle of frost
on the pavement

the turnip lantern –
his head is empty
his light shines out
through his face

black thoughts in my head –
three crows come out
of the *haar*

thick endless fog
the world is shrunk to a grey place
twenty yards across

the call and call of
invisible seagulls
in the fog

cats quarrelling
outside my window –
the long cold night

something has gone wrong –
the workmen stand and stare
in the cold rain

the tiny light flashes –
a message on the machine:
he died last night

the wind blows
a single note
on an empty bottle

remembering
my father's death—
cold november rain

winter sunshine
the washing on the line
is frozen stiff

morning meditation,
so cold we can see our breath,
chanting aum

mouse-tracks
across the frozen lard
in the frying pan

cold rain at the window
the only child
scolds her doll

the smile on the lips of
a dead cat by the roadside
this winter day

december afternoon
the light in the room
is cold and tired

rain on my birthday
another year more
another year less

the grey sky
snow falling into
the grey sea

gladness
on this wet winter morning
to be washing my bowl

skimming a stone
across the frozen pond
to hear it sing

in the snow-covered field
blue
a plastic milk-crate

last day of another year
bells
first day of another year

opening the window
to look out at
the new year

snow falling
everything
in its place

walking in the snow –
biting
into an apple

epiphany –
taking down the christmas cards,
the bare mantelpiece

fresh-fallen snow
not yet trodden by
anyone's feet –
I'll charge across!

the winter beach –
children building
snowcastles

driving sleet,
a street-light flickers
on and off

another night –
moonlight and roses
on my neighbour's accordion

astonished
to find myself
here

the snowman
calmly awaiting
the thaw

the incense stick burns down –
a heap of ash
the fragrance